# ATTACK OF THE...

# PESKY PARASITES

By William Anthony

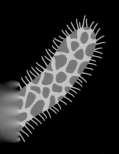

Enslow
PUBLISHING

Published in 2021 by Enslow Publishing, LLC
101 W. 23rd Street, Suite 240,
New York, NY 10011

Cataloging-in-Publication Data

Names: Anthony, William.
Title: Pesky parasites / William Anthony.
Description: New York : Enslow Publishing, 2021. | Series: Attack of the... | Includes
glossary and index.
Identifiers: ISBN 9781978519992 (pbk.) | ISBN 9781978520011 (library bound) | ISBN
9781978520004 (6 pack)
Subjects: LCSH: Parasites--Juvenile literature. | Parasitism--Juvenile literature.
Classification: LCC QL757.A584 2020 | DDC 577.8'57--dc23

CPSIA compliance information: Batch #BS20ENS: For further information contact Enslow Publishing, New York, New York at 1-800-542-2595

# PHOTO CREDITS

All images courtesy of Shutterstock. With thanks to Getty Images, Thinkstock Photo and iStockphoto.

Used throughout (including cover) – chekart (background), Sonechko57 (slime), VectorShow (microbe characters), Alena Ohneva (vector microbes), Olga_C (circle image frame). Used throughout (excluding cover) – Photo Melon (clipboard), Lorelyn Medina (scientist characters). P4–5 – Yurchanka Siarhei, Rattiya Thongdumhyu, p6–7 – SNP_SS, svtdesign, p8–9 – Crevis, Rattiya Thongdumhyu, p10–11 – Francesco_Ricciardi, Ayah Raushan, Crystal Eye Studio, chanawutt13, CloudyStock, p12–13 – Juan Gaertner, yusufdemirci, p14–15 – Henri Koskinen, Pavel1964, mark smith nsb, Christoph Burgstedt, p16–17 – Lano La, Yana Alisovna, p18–19 – jiraphoto, Hans Hillewaert, p20–21 – Aksenova Natalya, vectopicta, p23–24 – Monkey Business Images, motorolka, Sudowoodo.

# CONTENTS

Words that look like <u>this</u> can be found in the glossary on page 24.

## TRICKY WORDS

**PARASITE** = singular (one parasite)

**PARASITES** = plural (many parasites)

**PARASITIC** = to do with a parasite or many parasites

# LITTLE AND LARGE

Many microorganisms are so small that we can't even see them. These tiny terrors live in and on our bodies, and we usually don't know they're there.

"Micro" means tiny. "Organism" means a living thing.

There are some things that live in and on us that are big enough to see. Some of these creatures can even be many feet long.

**FEET?**
Well, I won't be needing my <u>microscope</u> for those...

5

# PESKY PARASITES

A parasite is a creature that lives in or on another living thing, called the host. Parasites need a host in order to survive.

Does that hurt the host?

Parasites use the host to get food. They either feed directly on the host or they steal some of the host's food.

"That's theft! Someone call the police!"

Taking the host's food helps parasites to grow before they <u>reproduce</u>. This starts the parasite's <u>life cycle</u> again.

"They multiply?

ONE WAS ENOUGH!"

Some parasites are too small for us to see, and others can be gigantic. No matter their size, they can cause the host a lot of harm.

" Parasites sound awful. They just take, take, take.

SO SELFISH! "

9

# TONGUE-EATING LOUSE

All sorts of living things can be attacked by parasites. Some fish have to live with the tongue-eating louse.

" I... I can see its head! GROSS! "

The louse goes through the fish's <u>gills</u> and eats its tongue. Then, the louse grabs on, pretends to be the fish's tongue, and steals its food.

We couldn't have chosen a worse parasite to start with!

# TAPEWORMS

Humans are targets for parasites too. Tapeworms are a type of parasite that live in your intestines. Some tapeworms can be many feet long.

"I think I need to lie down."

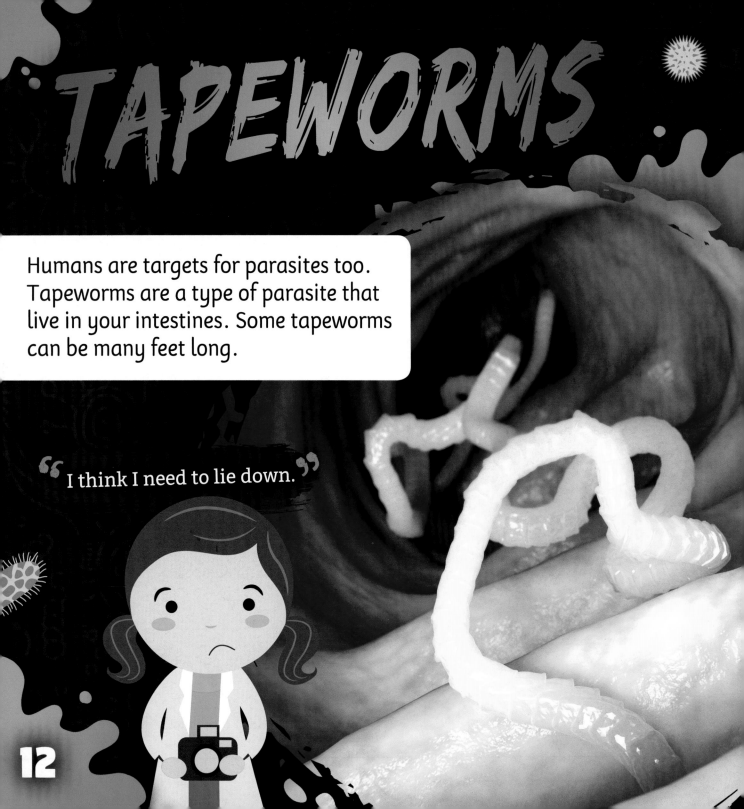

Tapeworms can have all sorts of bad effects on humans. They can cause:

- tummy pain
- diarrhea (runny poop)
- vomiting
- feeling more hungry or less hungry
- weight loss

"Thank goodness these things are <u>rare</u>..."

# GREEN-BANDED BROODSAC

The green-banded broodsac parasite turns snails into <u>zombies</u> to help it complete its life cycle.

"It's like we're living in a scary movie!"

14

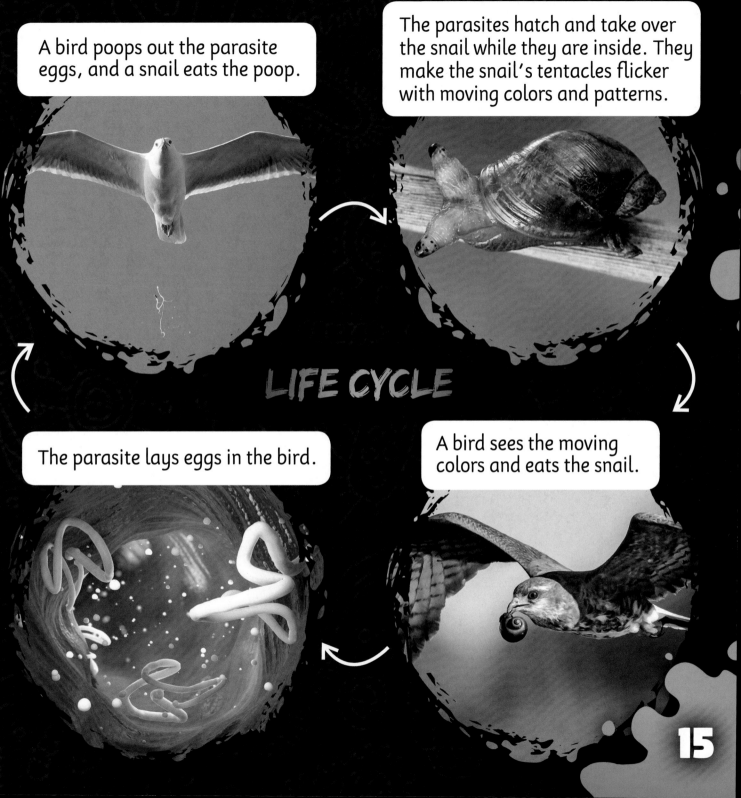

A bird poops out the parasite eggs, and a snail eats the poop.

The parasites hatch and take over the snail while they are inside. They make the snail's tentacles flicker with moving colors and patterns.

LIFE CYCLE

The parasite lays eggs in the bird.

A bird sees the moving colors and eats the snail.

# CORPSE LILY

Even plants can be parasites! The corpse lily is the largest flower in the world, but it has no leaves. Plants need leaves to make food.

Even the pretty parts of Earth can be evil? I'm off to live on Mars.

Because the lily can't make its own food, it steals <u>nutrients</u> from the roots of other plants. The flower is also one of the worst-smelling plants in the world.

"It's mean AND it stinks?
Why does this thing even exist?"

17

# SACCULINA CARCINI

Some parasites can completely control their host. *Sacculina carcini* is a barnacle that latches onto a crab and lays its eggs inside the crab's shell.

"Crabs are NOT puppets! Leave them alone, barnacle."

The barnacle then takes over the crab's entire body, including its brain. It turns the crab into a big babysitter for its newly hatched parasite babies.

"It can control the crab's brain? Not cool, barnacle. Not cool."

19

# TICKS

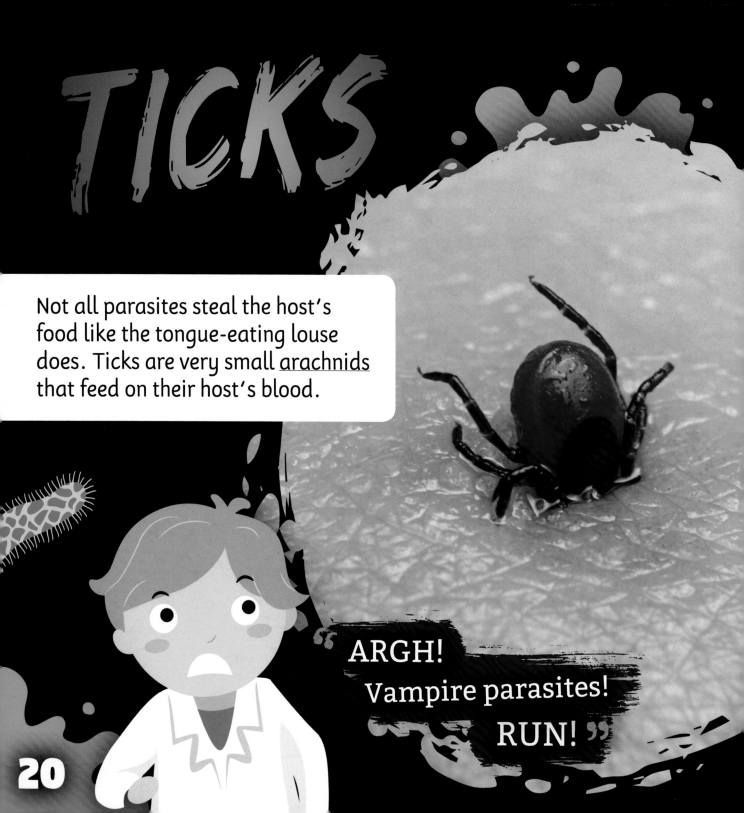

Not all parasites steal the host's food like the tongue-eating louse does. Ticks are very small <u>arachnids</u> that feed on their host's blood.

ARGH!
Vampire parasites!
RUN!

Ticks bite into the skin of animals to feed on the blood. Ticks are usually harmless to people and can be removed with tweezers.

"Usually harmless and easily removed? So, we can do something about parasites?"

TWEEZERS

21

# CREATURE COMBAT

Even inside our bodies, a parasite can still be beaten. Doctors can give us medicines that kill it or help us get rid of it naturally.

So, this is what "naturally" means...

Parasites on the outside of the body are just as easily removed. Like ticks, most can be pulled out of the skin. The war on parasites has begun!

Come at me, parasites.
I HAVE TWEEZERS!

# GLOSSARY

| | |
|---|---|
| arachnid | a type of animal that has eight legs, such as a spider |
| barnacle | a kind of small shellfish |
| gills | the organs that some animals use to breathe underwater |
| life cycle | the order of changes that a living thing goes through as it grows and develops |
| microscope | a piece of scientific equipment that makes things look many times bigger |
| nutrient | a natural thing that living things need to grow and stay healthy |
| rare | not common |
| reproduce | when a living thing creates a new living thing that is the same type as itself |
| zombie | a living thing that is controlled by something else |

# INDEX